Made in the USA
Las Vegas, NV
11 March 2021

19397691R00056